# FLY GUY PRESENTS:
## CASTLES

## Tedd Arnold

Scholastic Inc.

# For Prince Kai, Princess Gracie, and Prince Lowell—T.A.

## Thank you, Stephen Pow at Central European University and AnnMarie Anderson, for your contributions to this book.

Photo credits:

Photos ©: cover: Alexandre Fagundes De Fagundes/Dreamstime; back cover: Morseicinque/Dreamstime; 4–5: Andrew Ray/LOOP IMAGES/Getty Images; 6 top: age fotostock/Superstock, Inc.; 6 bottom: Patryk Kosmider/Shutterstock, Inc.; 7: Alexei Fateev/Alamy Images; 8 left: GUIZIOU Franck/hemis.fr/Getty Images; 8 right: IR Stone/iStockphoto; 9 left: Denny Rowland/Alamy Images; 9 right: Morseicinque/Dreamstime; 10 top: Carlos Soler Martinez/Dreamstime; 10 bottom: O6photo/iStockphoto; 11 top: VisitBritain/Britain on View/Getty Images; 11 bottom: DEA/G. GNEMMI/Getty Images; 12 top: Tamifreed/Dreamstime; 12 center: Hypermania37/Dreamstime; 12 bottom: Thomas Vieth/Dreamstime; 13 top: Heiko Bennewitz/iStockphoto; 13 center: Heritage Images/Getty Images; 13 bottom: Ihervas/Dreamstime; 14 top: Iskren Petrov/Dreamstime; 14 bottom: Geoff Dann/Getty Images; 15 top: mtcurado/iStockphoto; 15 center: North Wind Picture Archives; 15 bottom: Grafvision/Dreamstime; 16 top: Mary Martin/Science Source; 16 bottom: duncan1890/iStockphoto; 17 top: T33385 Abelard (1079–1142) and his Pupil Heloise (1101–63), 1882 (oil on canvas), Leighton, Edmund Blair (1853–1922)/Phillips, The International Fine Art Auctioneers, UK/Photo © Bonhams, London, UK/Bridgeman Art Library; 17 center: Boy with a Falcon and a Leash, c.1665 (oil on canvas), Noordt, Jan or Joan van (fl.1644–76)/© Wallace Collection, London, UK/Bridgeman Art Library; 17 bottom left: Heritage Image Partnership Ltd/Alamy Images; 17 bottom right: Print Collector/Getty Images; 18 top: Prince Edward, the Black Prince, being knighted by his father, King Edward III, English School, (19th century)/Private Collection/© Look and Learn/Bridgeman Art Library; 18 bottom: Tracy King/Dreamstime; 19 knight: Nejron/Dreamstime; 19 sword: Nejron Photo/Shutterstock, Inc.; 20 top left: Garry Platt/Flickr; 20 top right: Alinari/Art Resource, NY; 20 bottom right: eddyo2/iStockphoto; 20 bottom left: Otnaydur/Dreamstime; 21 top: DEA/ S. VANNINI/Getty Images; 21 bottom: Album/Prisma/Newscom; 22 top: StudioCampo/iStockphoto; 22 center: Philippa Banks/Dreamstime; 22 bottom: Culture Club/Getty Images; 23 top left: Linda Steward/iStockphoto; 23 top right: FOTOGRAFIA/iStockphoto; 23 bottom: DEA/G. NIMATALLAH/Getty Images; 24 top left: John Kellerman/Alamy Images; 24 top right: Angelamaria/Dreamstime; 24 bottom: villorejo/iStockphoto; 25 top: Marko Palm/Dreamstime; 25 bottom: Tupungato/Dreamstime; 26 top: Grand Ceremonial Banquet at the French Court in the 14th century, from a 19th century engraving in 'Dictionnaire du Mobilier Francais' by M. Viollet-Leduc, from 'Le Moyen Age et La Renaissance' by Paul Lacroix (1806–84) published 1847 (litho), French School, (19th century)/Private Collection/Ken Welsh/Bridgeman Art Library; 26 bottom: Zsolt Szabo/iStockphoto; 27 top left: digitalgenetics/Thinkstock; 27 top right: ruslan_100/Fotolia; 27 bottom: Dario Lo Presti/Thinkstock; 28 top: Sergey Kelin/Dreamstime; 28 bottom left: Sean Pavone/Dreamstime; 28 bottom right: Daniel Logan/Dreamstime; 29 top right: Anne Rippy/Getty Images; 29 top left: Gynane/Dreamstime; 29 center: Bruce M. Esbin/Getty Images; 29 bottom: Szefei/Dreamstime; 30 top left: bluejayphoto/iStockphoto; 30 top right: Mike D. Tankosich/Dreamstime; 30 bottom: Vlad Limir Berevoianu/Alamy Images; 31 center left: Oleksandr Chuklov/Dreamstime; 31 center right: Lukasz Janyst/Dreamstime; 31 bottom: Kmiragaya/Dreamstime; 31 top: MACIE J NOSKOWSKI/iStockphoto.

ISBN 978-0-545-91738-4

10 9 8 7 6 5 4 3 2 1     17 18 19 20 21

Printed in the U.S.A.    40
First printing, January 2017

Designed by Marissa Asuncion

A boy had a pet fly named Fly Guy.
Fly Guy could say the boy's name —

Buzz and Fly Guy were visiting a castle.

"Whoa!" said Buzz. "This place is amazing."

YEZZ!

Fly Guy wondered what it was like to live in a castle.

They headed inside to find out...

Castles are fancy homes.

Castles are fortresses, too. They are designed to keep those inside safe. They have defenses like drawbridges and gates to keep enemies out.

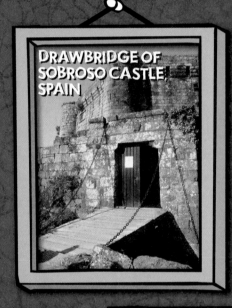

DRAWBRIDGE OF SOBROSO CASTLE, SPAIN

HALTZ!

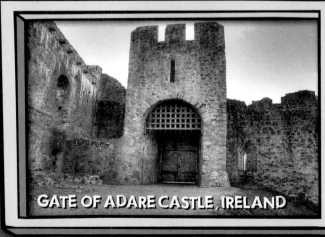

GATE OF ADARE CASTLE, IRELAND

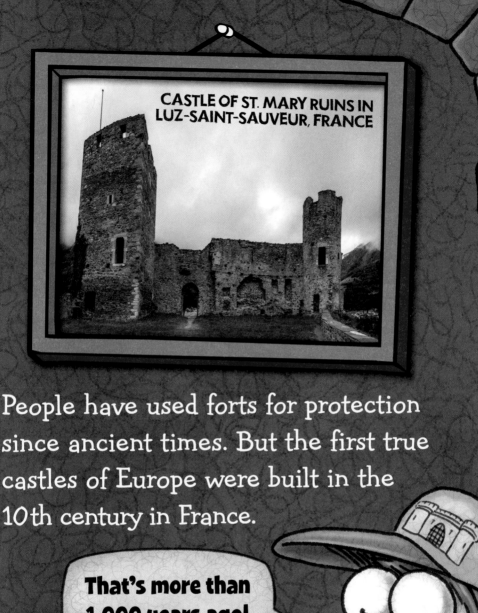

CASTLE OF ST. MARY RUINS IN LUZ-SAINT-SAUVEUR, FRANCE

People have used forts for protection since ancient times. But the first true castles of Europe were built in the 10th century in France.

That's more than 1,000 years ago!

Most of the castles we admire today were built in Europe during the Middle Ages (around AD 500–1500).

**HUZZAH!**

CHÂTEAU D'IVRY-LA-BATAILLE, FRANCE

TOWER OF LONDON, ENGLAND

**AROUND 950**

The first castles are built in France from earth and wood. Wood burns easily, so castles are soon built from stone. Most stone castles have walls that are at least 8 feet thick.

**1066**

William the Conqueror invades England from France and becomes king. He starts building the Tower of London—a large, square stone fortress.

CHÂTEAU DE SAUMUR, FRANCE

DOVER CASTLE, ENGLAND

**1180-1400s**

Many castles are built in France. These castles look fancier than English castles. Many have tall, round towers with cone-shaped roofs.

**1180**

Dover Castle in England is one of the first concentric castles. That means one ring of stone wall is built around another wall.

**The Middle Ages are also called the Medieval Period!**

If an enemy wanted to take over an area of land, they had to take control of the castle on that land. Every part of a castle's grounds was designed to keep the enemy from getting inside.

PARAPET:
A low wall around the top of a tower.

GATEHOUSE:
The main entrance.

A lookout point. Guards could see for miles from up here!

WATCHTOWER

KEEP:
The castle's
main building.

MOTTE:
A tall hill.

MOAT:
A deep ditch around the castle,
often filled with water.

OUTER CURTAIN:
The outer wall.

INNER CURTAIN:
The inner wall.

Castles were often attacked. So they had many defenses built into their walls.

A drawbridge could be raised to block enemies from entering the castle.

DRAWBRIDGE

PORTCULLIS

A portcullis was a heavy wooden or metal gate. It was lowered to keep enemies out.

Roofs were made of slate or tile to protect the castle from flaming arrows.

TILE ROOF

Crenels were tooth-like gaps in the parapet. Guards could keep an eye out for attackers.

CRENELS

Murder holes were holes in the ceiling. Guards used them to shoot arrows or pour boiling water or hot sand on enemies' heads!

MURDER HOLES

An arrow loop (or arrow slit) was a thin, vertical slit in the castle wall.

ARROW LOOP

Guards could safely shoot arrows at the enemy!

Attackers used different weapons to try to take control of the castle.

A mangonel was a catapult. It was used to throw heavy objects at castle walls.

MANGONEL

A trebuchet was a machine that flung objects like heavy stones, beehives, or animal poop up and over the castle walls.

TREBUCHET

That could throw a lot of poop! Yuck!

A ballista was a cross between a giant bow and a catapult. It was used to launch sharp, heavy darts at targets.

○ BALLISTA ○

A battering ram was a hanging tree trunk that attackers slammed into the castle's wooden gates.

BUZZ SAYS POOPZ!

○ BATTERING RAM ○

A siege tower was a tall wooden tower with wheels. Men pushed it close to the castle so they could climb over the wall.

○ SIEGE TOWER ○

Life inside a castle depended on who you were.

The king and queen ruled over everyone in the country.

There was a lot of land to protect. So the king often gave land to a rich friend, called a lord. As the king's friend, the lord was allowed to build a castle to protect that land.

The lord and lady lived in one of the castle's towers. Their children learned to read and write.

Boys might learn to play an instrument, ride horses, fly hawks, or play chess.

Girls learned to sing, sew, and help run the household.

Knights also lived in the castle. They worked for the ruler to defend the castle. A boy began knight training at age 7. When he turned 21, he became a knight.

A RULER TAPS A YOUNG MAN ON THE SHOULDER WITH THE FLAT SIDE OF A SWORD. THIS MAKES HIM A KNIGHT.

Horsefly

Knights rode horses into battle. They practiced their skills by jousting. Two knights raced toward each other carrying long wooden poles called lances. Each knight tried to knock the other off his horse first.

° JOUSTING °

A COAT OF ARMS LET OTHERS KNOW WHICH KING OR LORD THE KNIGHT FOUGHT FOR.

METAL HELMET

MAIL ARMOR WAS A LAYER OF TINY LINKED METAL RINGS. ARROWS COULDN'T POKE THROUGH IT!

SHIELD

A DAGGER WAS SHORTER THAN A SWORD. IT WAS USED FOR STABBING.

SWORD

A full suit of armor weighed as much as 3 bowling balls!

Servants and other workers lived in the castle, too. This included kitchen workers, gardeners, blacksmiths, tailors, priests, doctors, jesters or other entertainers.

KITCHEN WORKER

GARDENER

The blacksmith made horseshoes, tools, nails, and weapons.

BLACKSMITH

HORSESHOE

**TAILOR**

The tailor made clothing from wool or silk cloth.

The jester told jokes, played instruments, sang, juggled, and did magic tricks.

**JESTER**

Many pets lived in castles.

Cats kept rats and mice away.

Falcons or hawks
were trained
to catch small
animals.

Peregrine Falcon

Pigeons
sometimes
carried
messages to
other castles!

Dogs such as beagles were used to hunt rabbits.

Horses were used for travel, battles, hunts, and farmwork.

**FLIES LIVED IN CASTLES, TOO!**

Most parts of a castle were crowded, shared spaces.

Only the ruling family had its own rooms. These rooms smelled good because fresh herbs hung from the walls.

• LANGEAIS CASTLE, FRANCE •

• FRESH HERBS •

The castle toilet was called a garderobe. It was a wooden or stone slab with a hole in the middle. Waste fell down a chute. No one liked shoveling it out, but someone had to do it! This person was called the gong farmer.

• GARDEROBE •

The dungeon was often at the very bottom of the castle, below the basement. Some dungeons were rooms in high towers. Prisoners were held here.

The only way in or out was through a trapdoor in the floor.

Celebrations were held in the castle's main room—the great hall.

Fish from fish ponds or the moat might be served at a feast, along with beef and lamb. Wild birds would be baked into pies.

YUMZZIE!

Desserts included custards and fruit tarts. They were usually sweetened with honey.

○ FRUIT TART ○

○ HONEY ○

Food was eaten off plates made of wood or pottery. They were called trenchers. Sometimes stale pieces of bread were used as trenchers. Everyone had a spoon and knife, but there were no forks.

**Who needs forks?!**

○ TRENCHERS ○

There are castles—and buildings like castles—all around the world. Many of them were built after the Middle Ages.

The Kremlin in Russia has five palaces and four cathedrals.

Himeji Castle in Japan is known as "White Egret Castle." It looks like a beautiful bird!

Great Egret

Alcázar de Segovia in Spain looks like the bow of a ship.

Château de Villandry in France is famous for its gardens.

Lal Qila (or Red Fort) in India is named for its red sandstone walls.

CASTLEZ EVERYWHERE!

Castles have inspired the work of many artists and authors.

Neuschwanstein Castle in Germany inspired artist Walt Disney to build Sleeping Beauty Castle at Disneyland Park.

NEUSCHWANSTEIN CASTLE

SLEEPING BEAUTY CASTLE

BRAN CASTLE

Bran Castle in Romania is also called Dracula's Castle. Bram Stoker wrote *Dracula* in 1897. Many people believe this castle was his inspiration.

Castles today are often museums. Some are still home to modern families.

Prague Castle is the home of the Czech president.

PRAGUE CASTLE

WINDSOR CASTLE

Windsor Castle is the oldest castle in the world to still have people living in it.

At Blarney Castle, visitors kiss the Blarney Stone.

BLARNEY CASTLE

There's even a castle in New York City!

Belvedere Castle is actually a weather station.

"It was fun to learn about castles," Buzz told Fly Guy. "It's even more fun to make our own!"

Buzz and Fly Guy could not wait for their next field trip.